ELECTRONIC GAMES

BY FRED D' IGNAZIO

A GROLIER COMPANY

FRANKLIN WATTS
New York/London/Toronto/Sydney/1982
A FIRST BOOK

Cover photographs courtesy of Atari, Inc.

Photographs courtesy of Bell Laboratories: p. 3; Motorola Inc.: p. 8; Rosetta, Inc.: p. 11; Automated Simulations, Inc.: pp. 14 (top) and 44; Coleco Industries: p. 14 (bottom); Bally Consumer Products Division, Midway Manufacturing Company: pp. 18 and 57; Atari, Inc.: pp. 21 and 30; Mattel Electronics Division, Mattel Inc.: pp. 24 and 27 (World Championship™ Games); Tandy Corporation/Radio Shack: p. 34; Milton Bradley Company: p. 40; Magnavox/N.A.P. Consumer Electronics Corporation: p. 43.

Library of Congress Cataloging in Publication Data

D'Ignazio, Fred.
Electronic games.

(A First book)
Bibliography: p.
Includes index.
Summary: Discusses the development of electronic games, their basic operation and design, available accessories, rules of some of the most popular games, and the winning strategies of several champion players.
1. Electronic games—Juvenile literature.
[1. Electronic games] I. Title.
GV1469.2.D53   794   82-1962
ISBN 0-531-04396-7   AACR2

CONTENTS

For Sarah, Larry, Mark, and Ben:
Today's Master Gamers,
Tomorrow's Computer Wizards

ANNALS OF AKALABETH

Mondain, second born of Wolfgang,
a great king of old, wished to gain
his brother's inheritance, and so
he used his great powers for evil . . .

. . . He created deep dungeons, so deep
and extensive that the lower depths had
never been explored. In these dungeons
he unleashed more evil.
He sent thieves, skeletons, and snakes
to dwell near the surface, and
daemons and balrogs to guard the depths.
Now blood flowed freely in Akalabeth . . .

Mondain cast such sickness and
pestilence upon Akalabeth that both
man and beast lived in constant fear.
Thus was the Dark Age of Akalabeth.

Akalabeth is the name of a new electronic game
created by the California Pacific Computer Company.
You play *Akalabeth* on a small Apple computer.
When you begin the game, you "enter" the world
of Akalabeth. You become an ally of Lord British,
Champion of the White Light, and mortal enemy of
the evil Mondain. You can become a warrior or
a wizard, but once you enter the game, it is your
duty to "rid Akalabeth of foul creatures that infest it,
while trying to stay alive."

As you begin the game, a warning flashes on
the computer picture screen:

BEWARE FOOLISH MORTAL . . .
YOU TRESPASS IN AKALABETH!
WORLD OF DOOM . . .

Do you dare play the game?
This is your last chance to turn back.

CHAPTER 1

A BRIEF HISTORY OF ELECTRONIC GAMES

■ *The Shrinking Computer*

Everywhere you look — in game arcades, department-store lobbies, and at home — you see people playing electronic games. Since the games are "electronic," they must have lots of circuits and wires inside — and they do. But the most important circuits and wires belong to a tiny computer.

Computers are the "brains" of electronic games. Computers today are extremely small and inexpensive. But they used to be much bigger and cost a fortune. A little over twenty years ago, most computers were huge boxes, bigger than a freight car or a moving van. The computer's information and commands zipped through thousands of miles of colorful spaghetti-like wires.

The military was the largest user of computers in the early days. They used them to guide and control radar and other aircraft-tracking systems, submarines, airplanes, and guided missiles. Yet the big, bulky computers took up too much space, were expensive, and weren't very reliable. Military and civilian scientists figured that the only way to solve this problem would be to make computers smaller — much, much smaller.

Today's *microcomputers* are no bigger than a large dab of tooth-paste, yet they are a million times faster than the old computers and store thousands of times more information. They cost only a few pennies to make and can perform trillions of calculations without making a mistake. They also have fancy new abilities: they can talk, play music, and draw moving, cartoon-like pictures. They are no longer used just for rocket ships and guided missiles. They have become exciting "game machines."

■ *Spacewar*
What makes computers different from all other machines is that you can *program* them — feed them instructions. In fact, a new computer won't do anything until you tell it what to do.

People known as *programmers* have been telling computers what to do ever since electronic computers were invented, back in the 1940s. Programmers knew that computers were expensive and were only to be used for serious business, but they wondered if computers could also learn how to play games.

Scientists and inventors have long been fascinated by the idea of creating a machine with some sort of "artificial intelligence" built into its wires. Even before computers were invented they constructed machines that could play chess, and they built a horde of robotic mice, dogs, turtles, even humans. By the late 1950s and early 1960s, programmers who were supposed to be using their expensive computers only for work were also secretly programming them to play games. The computers were acquiring some artificial intelligence and were becoming tricky and challenging opponents.

Then in 1962 Steve Russell, a programmer from Cambridge, Massachusetts, invented *Spacewar*, an exciting game of humans and aliens blasting around the universe in spaceships, fighting battles. *Spacewar* became so popular among programmers that by the mid-1960s computers all over the United States had secret copies. Department heads were pleased that their computer programmers were putting in so many extra hours on the job. But the programmers weren't working. They were playing *Spacewar*.

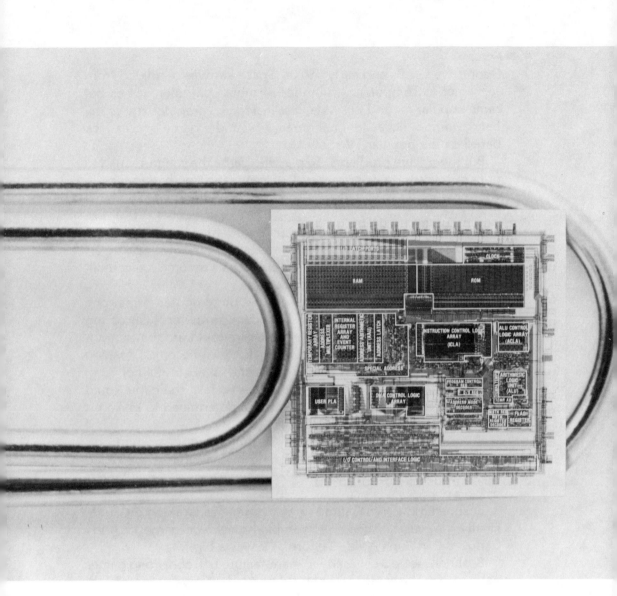

A miniature yet complete computer.
(Compare it to the size of the paper
clip.) Tiny computers are the "brains"
inside all electronic games.

■ Pong

During the 1960s and early 1970s, *Spacewar* was circulated from computer to computer. A number of other computer games became popular around this time, too, including computerized chess, backgammon, tic-tac-toe, hangman, life, and a game of *Star Trek* based on the popular TV show.

But there were problems. To play the game the computer had to print out words on its printer or TV screen, and you had to type in your next move. It was slow going, and everything was in words — no pictures.

In 1970, Nolan Bushnell, a graduate student at the University of Utah, was trying to write a new, improved version of *Spacewar*, and he was getting very upset. The game had become too complicated to play. Even worse, it was boring.

Bushnell began planning a new type of computer game, one that could be played on the new, miniature computers just coming on the market. He also wanted a game that could use the computer's newly acquired ability to draw moving pictures on a TV screen and that would be played with buttons and levers instead of typewriter keys. Since the new computer was so fast, the game could be fast — and exciting. Bushnell was also determined to make his new game simple to play and addictive.

With all these ideas in his head, Bushnell disappeared into his workshop and spent months designing his new game. He called the game *Pong*, since it was an electronic version of table tennis, or ping-pong.

Bushnell moved to California and continued working on *Pong*. Finally, he was finished. He took his homemade game to Andy Capp's Bar in Sunnyvale, California. It was a big hit.

Bushnell set up a company to manufacture barroom *Pong* games nationwide. The company's name was Atari. Five years after Bushnell founded the company, it had become the world's leading manufacturer of electronic games — including barroom, arcade, home video (TV), and hand-held games.

Bushnell was the inventor of the first nationally successful electronic arcade game. But credit for the first home video game goes to Ralph Baer, who in 1971 took his invention to Magnavox Corporation. The company bought it immediately, and in March 1972 unveiled Odyssey, the world's first commercial home video game machine. Odyssey was an overnight success, even though it was primitive according to today's standards. For example, when you hit the ball from the ping-pong game toward the edge of the TV screen, it didn't bounce back. It went right off the screen and disappeared.

By 1979, Magnavox was using powerful new microcomputers and had introduced Odyssey^2, a greatly improved version of its original game. Meanwhile, Atari had introduced home computers — machines you could program to create video games of your own.

If you got tired of inventing your own games, you could convert your home computer into a video game machine. Each computer had a slot for plugging in a game cartridge — a package of computer circuits inside a square, plastic shell. Stored in the cartridges were all sorts of electronic games, from chess and basketball to *Star Raiders*. *Raiders* was a fast-moving mixture of *Pong* and *Spacewar*, complete with sound effects, enemy zylons, and three-dimensional flights through outer space.

By the late 1970s, hundreds of thousands of people were playing electronic arcade games, home video games, and making up their own games on home computers. Then Mattel Toys introduced *Football* and *Auto Race*, the first electronic games small enough to fit into the palm of your hand.

■ *The New Games*
As computers got cheaper, smaller, and more powerful, electronic games got better and more sophisticated. Today, the fancy electronic arcade games make *Pong* look dull and tame by comparison. The newer hand-held games beep, flash, and talk.

You play the new home computer and video games using your color TV and game controls. There are also electronic board games and tabletop games with a tiny computer hidden inside. The most popular new electronic games let you pretend to be a wizard, knight, or beautiful princess and search for treasure in a haunted castle or battle a fiery dragon.

And the games keep improving. In the near future, you will play games with large (7-foot-high), flat TV screens and see incredibly realistic moving pictures in three dimensions and in color. You will be able to give orders to the game by wearing lightweight earphones and talking into a microphone. And by plugging your game into a telephone, you will be able to play in contests and tournaments with your friends long-distance. Your games may even talk to you and play music or come equipped with game robots!

CHAPTER
2

HOW ELECTRONIC
GAMES WORK

■ *The Game Computer*
If you took an electronic game apart, inside you would find a plastic board and, plugged into the board, a number of *integrated circuits*, or ICs, in flat, square cases. With their dozens of little metal legs, the cases look very much like fat, black caterpillars. Because of this, engineers often call them "bugs."

If you could pry off the top of each bug, you'd find the IC itself right in the center. If you took the IC and placed it under a microscope, you would see thousands of tiny, crisscrossing "canals" of silver flowing along miniature trenches. The trenches are etched by a needlepoint laser beam or X-ray beam into a square slice of silicon even thinner than one of the hairs on your head. Along these silver "wires" flash pulses of electricity that carry game information and commands to and from the computer.

Each IC has a special job to do. But one IC is the boss of all the others. This IC is the computer. It doesn't look any different from its neighboring ICs, but it is different. It oversees everything the game does from the moment you switch the game on.

The "bugs" plugged into the plastic
board of the computer. Riding atop
one bug is a tiny computer chip.

The computer may be on a single IC, or, in larger games, it may take up several ICs. In either case, it has three important parts — two kinds of memory and a "brain."

The first kind of memory is called *ROM* (*Read Only Memory*). On the ROM are stored the game rules and the strategies the computer follows to evaluate your moves and come up with moves of its own to try to beat you. All of the strategies and rules are permanently stored in the memory at the factory when the game is manufactured.

The second kind of memory is called *RAM* (*Random Access Memory*). The RAM acts like a scratchpad of paper. The computer "writes" (records) important information in RAM while the game is being played. For example, the computer uses RAM to remember your instructions and answers.

RAM also stores the computer's calculations and the status of everything in the game, including the computer's score, your score, the location of your player, the location of the computer's player, and so on. If you are playing a *Spacewar*-type game, RAM will also store how much fuel you have left and how many alien invaders you have blown up. If you are playing a football game, RAM stores the playing time left in each quarter, who has the ball, what down it is, the penalties, the scores, and so on.

The third part of the computer is the microprocessor, or the *CPU* (*Central Processing Unit*). The CPU is the computer's "switchboard." All information and commands must go through the CPU. The CPU can do arithmetic, so it handles the game's scorekeeping. It can keep time, so it runs the game's clock. It can recall information from both of the computer's (RAM and ROM) memories, so it remembers things like the rules and the locations of all the players. And it can make decisions. It can analyze your moves and attempt to come up with better moves that will help it defeat you and win the game.

In most cases, the CPU is incredibly fast. All information, numbers, commands, and decisions processed by the CPU are in the form of electrical pulses. These pulses race along at a speed only slightly less than the speed of light, which is about 186,000 miles, or 298,000 km, per second.

The computer inside an electronic game really isn't very intelligent. You're a lot smarter. But its speed makes up for its lack of intelligence. Speed helps the computer handle several parts of the game at the same time (including the sounds, picture display, scorekeeping, timekeeping, and playing) and enables the computer to calculate its next move in the blink of an eye. Speed, not intelligence, turns the computer into a tough opponent.

■ The Game Display

The computer creates the pictures you see in an electronic game. To understand how it does this, let's first think about window screens.

Find a window screen and look at it up close. What do you see? Lots of tiny wires, right? Half the wires go up and down. The other half go across the screen. All the crisscrossing wires create thousands of tiny squares, all arranged in neat little rows from the top of the screen all the way down to the bottom.

A game's picture screen is a lot like this. Even though different kinds of games use different kinds of displays, they all resemble a window screen in that they are all divided up into hundreds or thousands of little squares.

Each of the little squares is called a *pixel*, for "picture element" or "picture cell." The game computer can fill each pixel with white light or with a color. The computer draws the pictures for the game by lighting up pixels all over the screen with different colors or white. All the little colored (or white) pixels together become pictures of the race cars, asteroids, dragons, or football players you battle or control in an electronic game.

The computer can also draw pictures in a different way. In string art, you take a board, paint it, and hammer nails into the board in some geometric shape or pattern. Then you take some thread and stretch it from one nail to the next. Pretty soon you have a compli-

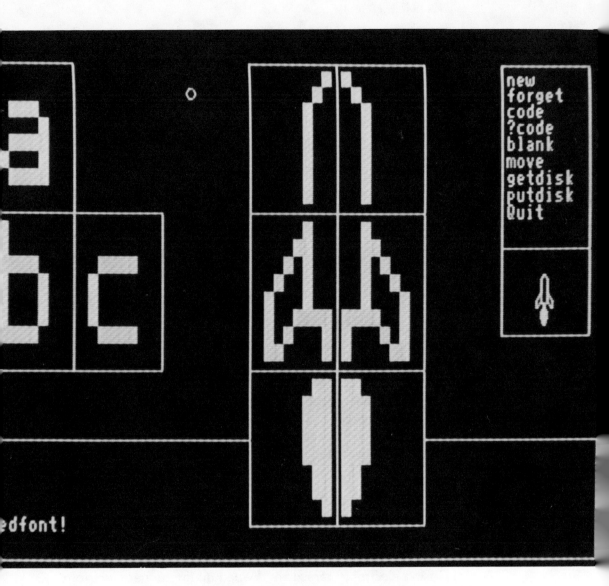

*The computer builds its pictures by lighting up
tiny blocks of light on the screen.*

cated design made up of lots of little straight lines of thread zig-zagging all around the board.

The computer can make pictures in a similar way. These pictures — 3-D outlines of spaceships, tanks, aliens, and castles — are called "wire frames" because they look like they were made from wire (or thread). They look complicated, but they are made from a very simple technique — lots of little straight lines. To make even the most complicated picture, the computer starts by selecting two points on the screen. Then it connects them with a straight line. Then it selects a new point and draws a new line that connects the end of the old line with the new point. Try this yourself. Try to draw a picture of a rocket ship by connecting points and drawing only straight lines.

But wait. Isn't there a problem? If you can only use straight lines, how do you draw curved surfaces like a dragon's tail or the edge of a flying saucer? How do you draw something circular, like a planet?

The answer is that you use very small straight lines — lots and lots of points very close together connected by very small straight lines. Try it with a circle. First draw a circle using only eight points and connecting them with straight lines. What shape do you get? You should get an octagon, an eight-sided figure. An octagon looks sort of like a circle, but it is too blocky.

Next draw a circle using twice as many points — sixteen. You end up with a sixteen-sided figure. It is still not a real circle, but it looks more like a circle than your octagon did.

You get the idea. If you now used 64 points or 128 points, put them really close together, and connected them with straight lines, you would have something that looks a lot like a circle, unless you looked up close. The more points you used, the better your circle would look.

Screens on electronic games are divided up into either pixels or points, and the game computer draws a picture either by coloring in pixels or by connecting points with straight lines. Either way, the more pixels or points, the better the picture. If there are only a few pixels or points, the game figures look blocky, jagged, and not very realistic. But if there are lots of pixels or points, the game figures look so real they could jump right out at you.

Yet what makes an electronic game realistic and exciting is not just the number of points or pixels. It's also the movement — the action. Race cars have to twist and turn along a narrow track. Dinosaurs have to lumber after fleeing humans. Asteroids and space invaders must hurtle across the screen threatening to blow your game ship apart. How does the computer make the pictures move?

Computers make game pictures move the same way cartoonists make their cartoons move. They draw lots and lots of "still" pictures called *frames*. Each frame is almost exactly the same as the one before it, but not quite. In each frame, the spaceships, the trolls, or the hockey players have moved just a tiny bit. Then in the next frame they have moved a tiny bit more.

The computer creates an illusion of motion — of action — by creating hundreds of frames and flashing them on the screen, one after another, really fast. For example, a computer may draw and erase thirty frames of an enemy submarine in a single second. But you don't see thirty separate pictures, each of a submarine standing still. Instead your eyes are fooled into seeing a single, moving picture of a submarine gliding across your screen.

How do you, as a game player, control these pictures? You control them by sending messages to the computer. All the buttons, switches, and dials on the game are computer "hot lines." For example, in a space-war game, you hit the THRUST button to get your spaceship to blast forward. By pushing this button, you are actually telling the computer to draw a new sequence of pictures, one that will create an illusion of your ship zooming across the screen.

■ *Sound Effects*
How does your electronic game make the sound of an explosion? How does it beep, whistle, and make noises like police sirens, roaring race-car engines, and skidding tires? How does the game

Many games are
played by plugging
in a tape cassette
(left) or game
cartridges (below).

play fight songs like you hear at a real football game? How does the game talk?

The computer creates speech, sound effects, and music electronically, out of little charges of electricity. Stored in the computer's memory are all the voices, noises, and songs that are in a game computer's repertoire.

Each sound is planned to always appear at a certain point in a game. For example, after each goal in a soccer game, the soccer-stadium crowd makes a loud cheer. When a certain sound or group of sounds is needed, the computer goes to its memory and makes a copy of the electrical charges that, in code, represent the sound. Then it sends those charges through a device that decodes them and turns them into pulses of electricity. These pulses are then sent to a speaker, causing it to vibrate and producing sound waves that travel through the air.

■ *Game Cartridges*

Home computer games often have a master unit with typewriter keys or switches, game levers ("joysticks"), dials, and buttons ("game paddles"). To play a particular game, you plug the master unit into a tape cassette recorder and choose a game cassette. The game is stored on the magnetic tape as a sequence of game instructions and rules to the computer. When you press the PLAY button on the cassette, the game gets loaded into the computer's memory. To begin the game, you might press a START button, type RUN, or the game might begin automatically.

Many games don't come on tape cassettes, which tend to be slow and sometimes unreliable. Instead, they come on (ROM) memory chips inside plastic game cartridges. You insert the game cartridge into a slot in the master unit. The computer inside reads in the game instructions from the game-cartridge memory chip at high speed, and the game instantly begins.

CHAPTER 3

WATCH OUT FOR FLYING MOUNTAINS!

■ *Pinball*

Pinball is the "old man" of electronic games. It first got its start way back in the 1930s. Over the years, it became enormously popular. From the mid-1930s on, millions of people were playing pinball machines with names like *Man 'n the Moon* (1935), *The Wizard* (1937), and *Flying Saucers* (1950).

The paintings on the pinball machines' "backglass" (where the scores are displayed) were wild and exotic. Horrible aliens with wriggling tentacles slithered after beautiful women, and flying saucers fought spectacular battles near ringed planets with multiple, multicolored suns.

Yet despite pinball's popularity and the elaborate artwork on each machine, the insides of the machine evolved very slowly. Pinball machines of the early 1960s were not much different from those of the 1930s.

Then came the revolution in miniature computers and microelectronics. By the late 1970s, pinball machines had changed radically. The fantastic artwork is still there. And the pinball machine is still limited to a silvery ball bouncing its way around an obstacle path of buzzers, spinning doors, flippers, and holes.

But the new games, stuffed with modern electronics and tiny computer brains, come with a whole lot more. For example, one game, *Black Knight*, comes with thirty-two sounds, all generated electronically. When you put in your quarter, the Black Knight "comes alive" and challenges you to a pinball joust. In a deep, threatening voice he cries, "I will slay you, my enemy!" During the game you hear galloping hoofs, a bell, and explosions. When you miss a chance to save your ball, the Knight mocks you with a scornful, maddening laugh.

■ *Arcade Video Games*
Designers of pinball machines are now experimenting with games that have several flippers and several balls, all whizzing and buzzing around three or more different levels. The levels will be connected by chutes, ramps, elevators, trapdoors, and pogo-stick springs. Some games come in new X shapes that allow as many as four players to battle each other at the same time.

Yet in spite of clever new designs, pinball machines are losing ground to a new, more powerful opponent — the all-electronic arcade video game. The pinball machine has been around for fifty years, the video game less than ten. But the excitement and challenge that video games offer cannot be beat. In 1980, the video games for the first time edged ahead of pinball machines as game arcades' biggest moneymakers.

Veteran game players refer to each video game played as a "life." This life may be very brief if the game is particularly tricky or difficult. But it can be incredibly challenging and exciting. To survive in the world simulated in the video game, you have to concentrate intensely, or the buzzer sounds and "GAME OVER" flashes on the screen. You can get knocked off the machine in seconds.

When you play a new arcade video game for the first time, the machine is liable to beat you swiftly and shamefully. It may ex-

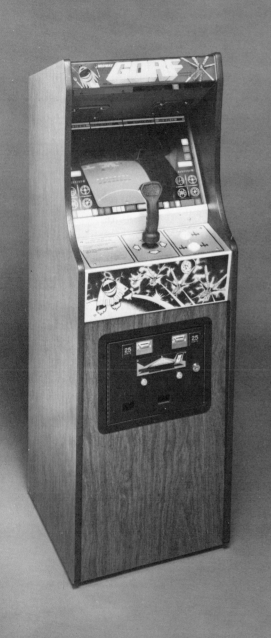

tinguish your "life" just like you were a gnat getting smacked by a flyswatter.

But soon you develop a hunger to prolong your life in the machine's fantasy world. You learn to master the game controls and how to outsmart the machine and all the hordes of aliens, monsters, asteroids, and spaceships that the machine throws at you.

And you learn to take risks. You abandon all caution and go for broke. Only the big score will do. By earning a big score you prolong your fantasy-world life. On a single quarter, you build your lifetime up from a few seconds to a few minutes to a half-hour, and maybe even to an hour. But you pay a price. As you get better, the computer gets trickier, and the action speeds up. You have to use every bit of skill and concentration you can muster to hang in there and fight back.

You forget all the noise and other people around you. You are totally inside the world of the game. One second of distraction, one *tiny* second of not paying attention, and the computer sneaks up behind you and wipes you out.

Video games are popular because of the challenge and excitement they offer and the fanatic concentration they demand. Yet this strength is also their weakness.

Look at the games lining the wall of one of your local arcades. How many games do you see that have been there for more than a year?

The answer, in most cases, is very few. The lifetime of even the best coin-operated video game is under six months. The reason? After a couple of months, people who constantly play the game get too good.

As your game-playing skills increase, two things happen. First,

Two models of the popular arcade video game, Gorf.

■ 19 ■

the challenge of the game fades. It is no longer as exciting as it was at first. And it is unlikely you will want to waste your money on a boring game. Second, as you get better, you stay on the machine longer. This means you aren't spending as much money. The machine is in use, but the waterfall of change into the coinbox has dried to a trickle. A machine with a partly filled or bare coinbox can't earn its keep. Arcade owners can't afford to hold onto an unprofitable machine. They must constantly replace all the "beaten" machines with new, more challenging ones.

New video games seem to come in waves, with one every now and then creating great excitement. The first really popular game was *Pong* in 1973. Atari's *Asteroids* game, which came out in 1979, was another hugely successful video game.

But the biggest new game in video game history came with the arrival of *Space Invaders* from Japan in 1978.

Pinball machine manufacturers usually sell only about 30,000 units of a particular machine. In only a couple of years, Taito Corporation, the creators of *Space Invaders*, sold over 300,000 *Space Invader* arcade games worldwide.

The introduction of arcade video games caused many new clubs to be organized and tournaments set up. Today, the best game players gather in different cities around the world to do battle for large cash prizes on speeded-up versions of the most popular games. Players routinely build up huge scores and stay on the machine for hours. New scoring and endurance records are made and then quickly broken.

A lot of people say video games are just a fad, that interest in them will soon die out.

It is true that video games will only remain popular as long as they are challenging and novel. But video game technology, unlike pinball technology, is almost entirely electronic and computerized. Electronic circuits are continuing to get smaller and computers fancier. As a result, amazing new video games are already on the horizon. They will be far more challenging and realistic than today's games.

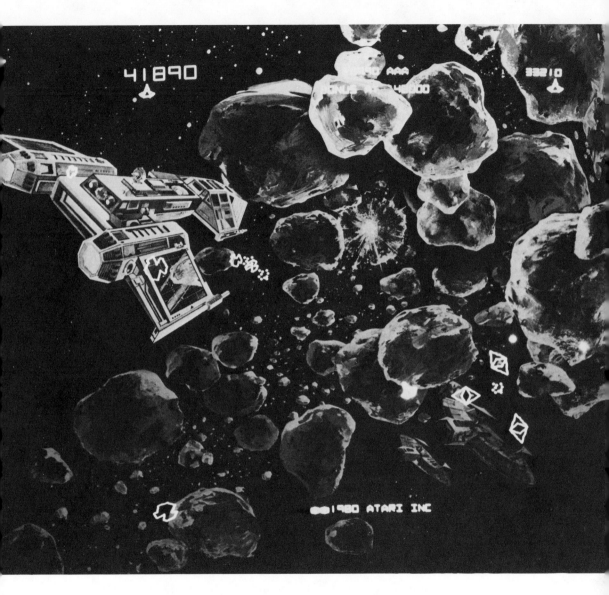

Newer arcade games feature fancy 3-D pictures,
sound effects, and multiple skill levels.

Right now, game designers are experimenting with new game ideas and new game equipment. The old video games were all along the lines of *Pong* or *Space Invaders* — batting around a blip of light on the screen or blasting onrushing aliens in outer-space shootouts. Newer video games are appearing with a variety of new approaches, though most still simulate life-and-death battles. For example, in one new game you fight in a tank war with a display that makes you feel like you are the driver of the tank. In another game you can pilot a spaceship and make attacks on an alien fortress surrounded by protective rings and "smart" killer mines.

Certain games, like Williams Electronics' *Defender*, are already very realistic. They feature long-range scanners; broken, irregular terrain; a joystick and a thrust button; hyperspace; humanoids; and "smart" bombs. The aliens attack your spaceship with bloodthirsty ferocity. And when you blast one of their ships, it explodes into a swarm of miniships that regroup and attack you again.

In the near future, the sound effects in the games will also be more realistic, and screen displays will feature full-color pictures. After that will come video games in three dimensions. Already Atari, in its *Asteroids Deluxe* game, is using a technique it calls "Quadriscan." The game bounces a realistic painted image of deep space off an overhead mirror onto the display screen. This creates the illusion of three dimensions.

Game designers are also experimenting with holographic images created from laser beams. In the future, when you pop your change into an arcade video game, you really will enter a fantasy world. When you step inside the game booth, three-dimensional asteroids, aliens, or monsters will surround you!

CHAPTER
4

FOOTBALL AT THE
BREAKFAST TABLE

■ *Board Games*

Nearly 5,000 years ago, an unknown Sumerian invented back-gammon, a game played on a clay tablet. Two thousand years later, Greek soldiers played checkers while the city of Troy burned. In India, the people's favorite was chess. In Rome, the rage was gambling — with lopsided dice.

Backgammon, checkers, and chess are, of course, still popular. And now, they are computerized! A tiny electronic opponent has replaced the live game players of ancient times. Inside the game, a small computer "brain" declares the odds, enforces the rules, and challenges you to hours of exciting, unpredictable contests. And checkers, chess, and backgammon are just three of a number of popular computerized board games.

At first, most of these games resembled calculators with odd-looking buttons. By pressing these buttons you entered your next move into the game. The game computer figured out its move and printed it on a tiny, calculatorlike display screen. You played the game using a regular game board and moved your game pieces and the computer's pieces around after each move.

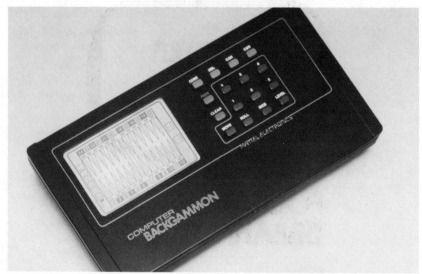

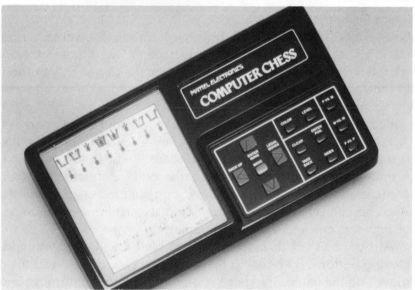

The computer that controls these electronic versions
of popular board games can battle you like an
expert or instruct you like a patient teacher.

Compared to the new electronic board games, these old games resemble a rickety Model T automobile. For example, some new games actually speak to you and tell you what their next move is. But they also insult you and try to fool you!

You can play a number of games on any one of ten different skill levels, from Novice to Master. If you press the SAVE GAME button, the computer will let you stop a match and return to it several days later. The computer can even turn into a teacher and help you become a better player. With a push of a button, the computer will lead you through dozens of famous moves or do an instant replay of your own game. And it will never tell anyone if you made a mistake.

The new electronic board games still have playing boards, but electronic ones. Some are touch-sensitive. In these, the computer can "feel" you move the game pieces around and always knows their locations. Other games are played on a touch-sensitive *LCD* (*Liquid Crystal Display*) screen. To move your piece, you just touch its image on the screen, then touch a new location. In a flash the computer moves your piece, then instantly moves its own piece.

There are even computers capable of playing lots of different games. You just plug in the right game cartridge and the computer will battle you in checkers, chess, Reversi (*Othello*), *Kriegspiel*, or blackjack.

A number of companies have built computer-controlled robot arms for their board games. When it is the computer's turn to move, the robot arm reaches out and moves its game piece. At the end of some games, the robot arm clears the board, then puts all of the pieces back on the board to begin a fresh match. And if you win the game, one robotic chess player tells you, "Congratulations!" and reaches out and shakes your hand.

■ *Hand-held Games*
Hand-held electronic games first appeared in 1977. Within three years, the number of hand-held games went from two to over four hundred.

■ 25 ■

Originally, hand-held games had tiny red *LED* (*Light-Emitting Diode*) displays with dots of light representing everything from weird alien invaders to hulking football players. The display was mounted on a calculator-type body. You could never play a friend, just the computer.

Today, few games look like calculators. There are games that fit into your pocket or come inside your wristwatch, tabletop games, and games that let as many as three people play all at the same time. The games play music, have realistic sound effects, and feature picture screens with real-looking aliens, spaceships, football players, and playing fields. Many game screens are touch-sensitive, so you no longer have to bother with buttons. You place a fingertip on a player or on the "menu" on the screen, and the computer responds instantly. In one game, for example, an angry dragon pursues your fingertip through a maze. Your fingertip "player" has to stay within the maze walls on the display screen, but the dragon can leap over the walls and chomp you.

Perhaps the best hand-held games are the sports games. Coleco's "head-to-head" baseball game lets you play a friend. It features realistic-looking players with batting averages. The players can bunt, hit and run, tag up, steal, and get thrown out on double plays. Pitchers throw a wide variety of pitches, including fast balls and curves. The computer begins each new contest with the song, "Take Me Out to the Ballgame." Other Coleco "head-to-head" games are equally realistic.

Mattel, too, has some excellent sports games. The tabletop "world championship" games feature large display screens with game players who wear color-coded uniforms so you can easily tell the teams apart. The games can be played at four different speeds and allow you to play manager and select "today's" players from a club roster complete with playing statistics for each team member.

In "world championship" football, you can control the quarterback and run plays with primary or secondary pass receivers or choose between any one of five offensive formations. On defense,

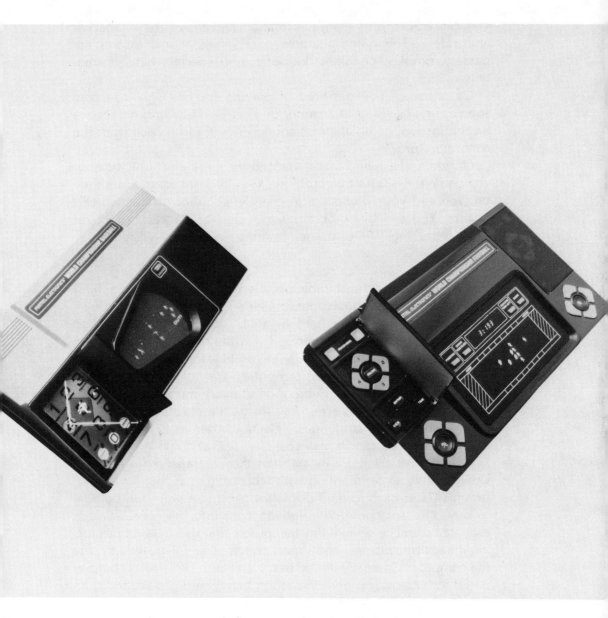

Some Mattel Electronics' hand-held games.

you can adjust your team's formation and move the linebacker and safety. The game features pass interceptions, incomplete passes, fumbles, penalties, kick-offs, and special "blitz" formations.

Of course, if you get tired of playing football, you can play soccer or go bowling. A number of electronic bowling games are on the market, complete with sound effects and advice from the computer "pro."

Or you and a friend might want to try some electronic boxing. The game starts with the traditional Gillette fight song. From then on, you and your friend are in complete control of the two LED boxers. You can block or throw punches or dance your boxer around the ring. The computer controls the boxing referee.

■ *New Games*

Hand-held, board, and tabletop electronic games are getting smarter as microcomputers get smaller and more powerful. In fact, they are getting so smart that they are being taken to national and international game tournaments. There they often defeat human experts and game programs running on big university computers. The reason is that the small computers are not general-purpose machines. They don't try to be good at everything, they just play games. Their programs are stored inside the machine in efficient, fast-moving game "languages." Electronic games that can defeat million-dollar computers may cost only $60 or $70.

New games are not only smarter, they are also more realistic. Designers are experimenting with tabletop games that have holographic (laser-produced) 3-D images. And you will soon be able to buy different game cartridges to plug into the games. Inside each game will be several tiny computers that specialize in producing the realistic pictures and sound effects. You will be able to play the computer Game Master or battle a friend. Either way, be prepared for explosions, photon cannon blasts, and growls and gunfire that look and sound startlingly real.

CHAPTER 5

INVADERS FROM SPACE

- *Home Video Games*

The first home video game didn't appear until 1972. Yet only eight years later, one of the leading video game manufacturers, Atari, had sold more than $300 million worth of game machines and game programs. To meet the fantastic demand, the company created more than forty game cartridges to plug into its game machine, the Video Computer System. On the cartridges were stored more than 500 games — all with sound effects, color pictures, and plenty of action.

With the rising cost of gasoline and entertainment outside the home, more and more people are buying video games and staying at home. Some people are even redesigning their living rooms and family rooms and converting them into home electronic entertainment centers — with large stereo speakers, a 5-foot (1.5-m) or 7-foot (2.1-m) TV screen, videodisk recordings of favorite movies, and, of course, a video game machine with a complete "library" of game cartridges. The cartridges contain electronic games for the entire family — games like *Combat, Breakout, Street Racer, Video*

*The Atari Video Computer System
with many of its game cartridges.*

Chess, Miniature Golf, Championship Soccer, Casino, and *Human Cannonball.*

What does the basic video game look like? A video game is different from an arcade game, a hand-held game, or a tabletop game in two important respects. First, full-scale TV video games often come with better pictures and sound than most other games. They also come with more playing options. For example, *you* choose the number of players, the skill level, and so on.

The second major difference is that most of the other games come in one self-contained unit. You just switch the power on and play. But a video game comes in pieces. There is the game console (or "master unit"), which contains the computer. There is the family TV set (a big color TV is best). There are also numerous kinds of game boxes. On top of these boxes are buttons, dials, and levers for controlling the action in the game.

Then there is a joystick controller, which looks a lot like a fancy stick shift in a sports car. You can grab the joystick and shift it in any of eight directions. The joystick lets you control most kinds of games, including sports games, maze games, space-war games, and so on. When you push or pull the joystick, your spaceship, football player, or dragster moves across the TV screen.

Most video games also come with a paddle controller, which either resembles a dial on your TV or a miniature car steering wheel. The paddle lets you move objects that only have to go in two directions (from right to left or left to right). There are also keyboard controllers, which are large and resemble an electric typewriter or are small and look like a calculator. Many games, in addition, come with plastic "masks" that slip over the keys of the keyboard controller. These masks identify each key's function within the context of a particular game. For example, on a *Spacewars* mask, the bottom righthand key might be labeled "SHIELDS." You push the SHIELDS button to raise your spaceship's protective shields in case of enemy attack.

When you first bring your video game home from the store, you can't just turn on the power and play. First you have to connect all the different parts. You have to plug the joystick (or other) controller into the master console and attach a master console video cable into the antenna slots of your TV. Next, you need to choose a game cartridge and plug it into the master console's game slot. And last, you need to plug the master console's power cord into a household electrical outlet.

Once your game begins, can you leap right into the action? Not yet. First you need to flip some switches on the master console. Among other things, these switches let you choose a black-and-white display or one in color and the skill level for the current game. Now, at last, you're ready to play.

Twisting, turning wires and cables, like a family of snakes and flatworms, connect all the different pieces in today's home video games. But not so in the future. Atari and other game manufacturers have already introduced remote controls that eliminate the messy connections.

Video games are so popular they have inspired bumper stickers, T-shirts, and video game books. It is not surprising that there are also video game tournaments and contests where the best players from a city or state, or the whole country, gather together and fight each other (and the computer) for the honor of being "number one."

In the fall of 1980 one such contest took place in New York City at the headquarters of Atari's parent company, Warner Communications, Inc. The occasion was the First National *Space Invaders* Competition. And the five finalists who arrived to do battle with the computer were chosen from over 10,000 *Space-Invader* players from all over the nation.

At exactly 10 A.M. on November 10, the day of the contest, the five young *Space-Invader* experts sat down together, shoulder to shoulder, in front of a row of Atari Video Computer System consoles and big color TV sets. The buzzer sounded and play began. Immediately the contest room was filled with sounds of booming explosions and laser-beam zaps.

One contestant, Steve Marmel, became overexcited, lost control, and was blown up after only 40,000 points. The other players survived for two grueling hours against wave after wave of attacking aliens.

When the cosmic debris had cleared, the scores on the TV sets indicated the clear winner and holder of a new world record. The winner, sixteen-year-old Bill Heineman of Whittier, California, had chalked up an incredible score of 165,200 points.

■ *Home Computer Games*
One problem with regular home video games is the small number of good game cartridges. The leading video game companies — Atari, Mattel, and Magnavox — are constantly introducing new games. But no matter which company's master console you have, you can only use that company's game cartridges. None of the others will work. If you are an active, enthusiastic game player, before long you will master all the games that appeal to you. They will become boring, and you'll give up playing them.

Fortunately, the game manufacturers themselves have come up with a solution. If you are a serious video game player, you can "graduate" from a regular video game to a home computer.

Programmable home computers may cost $500 or more. This makes them far more expensive than video game machines, which cost from $100 to $200 or so. But home computer prices are falling. For example, some of the newer models, such as the VIC-20 and TRS-80 Color Computer, cost less than $400. And one computer, the ZX-81, from Sinclair, is $200 already assembled and $100 if you build it from a kit.

If you do decide to get a home computer, the door to a new world of games opens before you. You no longer have to depend on the game manufacturer to supply you with new games. There are dozens of game factories springing up all over the country, churning out hundreds of games for small home computers such as the Apple, Atari, VIC, and Radio Shack Color Computer. The games come on tape cassettes, floppy disks, and on game cartridges. Many of them are of very high quality and promise you hours and hours of new challenges and excitement. Some, like *Gorgon*, from Sirius Software, resemble popular arcade games.

Here, electronic chess is being played
on a Radio Shack Color Computer.
Note that the game cartridge is plugged
into the computer's side.

But if you are a true "hard-core" video gamer, you still won't be satisfied. As you play the games, you will find yourself thinking up game variations that the game inventors never considered. You may even lie in bed at night and dream up ideas for new games that are twice as exciting as any you have ever seen.

Also, commercial games are expensive, usually from $10 to $40 apiece. You probably can't afford to buy new games as fast as you master the old ones.

What can you do? If you own a home computer you can stop buying "canned" games from other people and start inventing your own. The basic feature that makes a home computer different from a regular video game is that a home computer is programmable. This means you can write your own programs — game programs or programs of any kind.

Programming your own games gives you many advantages. You may, for example, be like a lot of other people who have played so many sports and space-war games that they are all starting to look alike. Most video games (for home computers or regular video game machines) are copies of very popular games that take place on a playing board (chess), in outer space (*Space Invaders, Asteroids*), or on a playing field (football, etc.). Why not try to think up some new games, with new rules and new heroes and villains, and have the action occur in a totally new location?

Remember, a home computer can be programmed to simulate (create a miniature replica of) anything going on in the real world or in any world you dream up. When you write a program, you make the rules. In your own games, why not begin in the crater of a volcano that is about to explode? Why not create a history game that lets you play the role of some great historical figure, such as Abraham Lincoln? Why not program a business game in which you can run a global, super-rich company like Exxon or IBM?

When you program your own games you get a chance to unleash your imagination and use the very latest game-design tools. The result may be a game that you can sell to a manufacturer. At the least, it will be something you and your family or friends can enjoy together for hours.

■ 35 ■

CHAPTER 6

REVENGE OF
THE UGLY TROLL

Imagine that you are in a castle cellar deep underground. A small candle on a box beside you casts murky, flickering light about the cramped, little room. Something in the room is dead and rotting. Its foul, decaying smell offends your nostrils and makes you feel sick.

The room's walls are covered by a dark green slime with orange splotches. Seeping in from the castle moat is oily, reddish-brown mud that oozes and gurgles around your feet. Under the mud lie nameless, hideous things. When you walk, your feet make crunching noises — like the sound of rat and bat skulls cracking.

You yank open a heavy metal door. A huge, ugly troll leaps on you, screaming and pounding you with a spiked wooden club.

The troll is all over you. "WHACK!" he smacks you in the side of the head. You see stars. You start to black out. It looks like this is the end.

But wait! Remember the black spider you took from the witch's cave?

You reach into your pocket, grab the spider, and hurl it at the troll. It lands on the troll's cap and, in a flash, weaves a web stronger than flame-treated steel around the troll's body. Lying in an ugly lump on the floor, the troll snarls at you as you leap over him and race out the door.

■ *Fantasy Role-Playing Games*

The scene just described is one you might find yourself in if you play fantasy role-playing games, or FRPGs. You can play FRPGs, such as the famous *Dungeons and Dragons* (invented in 1973 by Gary Gygax, now a trademark of TSR Hobbies), with a group of friends at home or in a tournament at a shopping mall. Or you can play them using the new tabletop FRPGs, put out by game manufacturers such as Mattel and Milton Bradley.

Or you might instead play an FRPG on a video game machine or home computer.

FRPGs have been around for about ten years. They grew out of war games and tales of King Arthur's court and the Middle Earth of J. R. R. Tolkien. And the games' monsters are cousins of the hideous creature Grendel, who terrorized the mythical England of Beowulf.

FRPGs are very popular today. Over 3 million people worldwide spend one or two nights a week setting up dungeons and embarking on perilous journeys into make-believe worlds.

FRPGs, at least non-electronic ones, require very little equipment. A Game Master creates each game fresh from his or her imagination and from the limited suggestions in the game manuals. Like a wizard out of the Dark Ages, the Game Master can create a world out of thin air. The Game Master often draws a map of this world, just to keep everything straight.

Next, each game player describes the character he or she has invented for the game. Sometimes the players wear costumes to make the game seem more real. Most players choose the traditional roles of cleric (religious leader), sorcerer, thief, or warrior.

Based on the fateful roll of oddly shaped dice, the players acquire such characteristics as beauty, strength, dexterity, intelligence, and experience, along with a variety of skills or other characteristics. The dice can even determine whether a player is lucky or destined to suffer misfortune.

The Game Master now reviews the inventory, or resources, the players are to carry with them or find during the course of the game. A player can't fight ugly trolls and clever sorcerers with just bare hands. He or she needs swords, guns, shields, lamps, and magic amulets. Needed also is money, in the form of jewels, gold coins, or precious art objects.

The Game Master explains some of the characteristics of the world the players will enter. Naturally, he or she avoids telling them about the traps, the unexpected detours, and the unpleasant surprises planted along the path. But one crucial thing is made clear: the goal, or mission. "Find the Lost Ring of Xandoor!" the Game Master may say, or "Rescue the Silver Prince from the dragon's lair!"

Finally, with the players gathered around, the Dungeon Master announces in a solemn voice, "Let the game begin!"

While in the make-believe world, the players are blind and deaf. The Game Master becomes their eyes, ears, and other senses. As they trudge along, stumbling from one adventure into another, the Game Master cleverly unfolds the details of the game world. One at a time, the bottomless pits, the fabulous treasures, and the hunger-crazed monsters are unleashed upon the players. The world slowly takes shape, with all its unexpected treasures and unspeakable horrors.

■ *Computer Adventure*

Game Masters need to be tricky and creative. They need to be pranksters and practical jokers. But most of all, Game Masters need to have wild imaginations. After all, inventing a new world isn't easy.

Game Masters always used to be human, but no longer. The new generation of Game Masters are electronic. They are computers with game worlds stored in their miniature, silver-threaded circuits.

Computerized FRPGs — known as adventure games — used to be played on big computers. But big computers shrank to the size of postage stamps and even smaller. Also, big computers were operated by companies and universities for serious business — payrolls, students' grades and test scores, income taxes, and so on. Playing games on a big computer was always frowned upon. Computer time and resources cost money. Many programmers who were caught playing on their company's computer were immediately fired.

Almost as soon as small home computers appeared, programmers began squeezing giant-sized adventure games into games small enough to fit into the home computer's tiny memory. Over the years, programmers got trickier and were able to fit more and more challenging games into a smaller amount of space. And as computers shrank even smaller, more and more computer memory became available for storing bigger and bigger games.

■ *Tabletop Adventure*
Computers are now so small and high-powered that an electronic adventure game can run on a transistor battery the size of a package of bubblegum. The game fits on top of a table. And inside a game board or plastic tower lurks the computer.

For example, in Milton Bradley's *Dark Tower*, your game world is in the form of a circular game board with an electronic tower at its center. To play, you press buttons on the tower keyboard. And, depending on the computer Game Master's command — in the form of sound effects, a digital display, and a lighted picture — you move dragons, warriors, castles, and flags around the game board.

Your mission is to win the kingdom. To do that you must find three magic keys, unlock the tower, and overcome the tower's defenders — before any of the other players. Each time you play, the computer Game Master comes up with a new adventure. The variety of games stored in the computer's memory keeps *Dark Tower* challenging and interesting.

Computer Game Masters also fit inside game boards. Mattel Electronics has a computer labyrinth game based on the non-computer version of *Dungeons & Dragons*. The labyrinth fits atop a plastic board, and the computer sits inside. One or two adven-

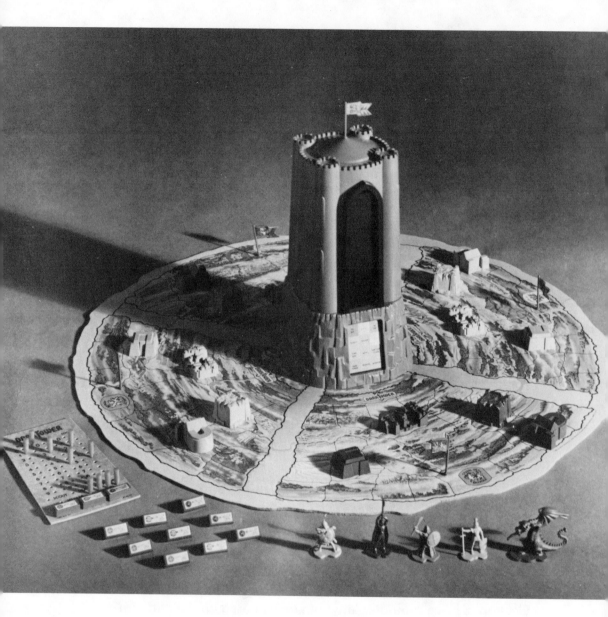

The new electronic adventure game, Dark Tower.

turous warriors wind their way through a twisting, turning maze in search of a hidden treasure. At any point they may encounter a deadly dragon, waiting silently around the corner.

The computer Game Master generates a new maze for each new game. It also creates sound effects.

The game can be played at two different skill levels. It is made especially challenging by the random shape of the maze and by a dragon that is both invisible and unpredictable. You never know where it will be hiding. Also, if an opposing player captures the treasure before you, you can sneak up on him or her in the maze, overpower the player, and steal the treasure for yourself.

■ Video Adventure

When adventure games first appeared on computers they resembled electronic books — all words and no pictures. The computer Game Master communicated with you by sending you messages in the form of moving lines of words flashing on the screen. Still, the games were fun because of the challenging riddles, puzzles, and situations created for you by the computer Game Master.

Video games arrived at the same time as computer adventure games (the early 1970s). These games were the opposite of adventure games. They were all pictures and no words. Video games were fun because of the fast action, the realistic sound effects, and the constantly moving, dazzling video displays.

In the early 1980s, the two types of games met and mixed together to form a new kind of game. The new games have the strategy, puzzles, and imaginative characters and situations of adventure games. And they have the sound effects and the fast-moving, animated pictures of video games. The combination can be spectacular.

Video adventure games can be played using only a video computer machine and a TV, or they can include a playing board with players and tokens. For example, to play Magnavox's *Quest for the Rings* game, you use a game board, a game cartridge, a master keyboard and console, joysticks, and your TV.

When you get everything hooked up and turn on the power you are instantly transported to "Alternate World," with its dangerous dungeons and its chilling crystal caverns. It is up to you and your team of game players to find and control the "Rings of Power" that lie concealed somewhere in the caverns. Guarding the rings are wizards, warriors, phantoms, changelings, and fire-breathing dragons.

Some video adventure games are played without a game board. All the action occurs on the TV picture screen. You type in game commands on the keyboard and use a joystick to move your players around on the screen.

In Mattel Electronics' enchanted maze game, for example, you assemble a team, choose your weapons, and descend into a netherworld maze of ghosts, sorcerers, and three-headed dragons. You watch yourself — an animated little figure on the screen — explore the treacherous passages of an underground maze, lighted in dim blue light. Hiding behind one of the creatures that block your path is the treasure you seek. Even if you defeat the creature and grab the treasure, you haven't won until you have discovered a way to escape from the maze.

■ *Home Computer Adventures*
There are hundreds of adventure games that you can play on any one of the popular home computers, including the Apple, Atari, Radio Shack's Color Computer, and Commodore's VIC-20. More and more of the games are stored on solid-state game cartridges. But most games still are stored on floppy disks or tape cassettes.

Home computer adventures are more varied than most video-game and tabletop adventures. There are, of course, lots of games featuring mazes, dragons, and dungeons. But there are also many other kinds of games as well. For example, in Automated Simulations' *Crush, Crumble and Chomp!*, you play the part of one of six different gigantic beasts, including a huge, winged carnivore, a hungry Tyrannosaurus rex, and a destroyer robot. You get to pick

Magnavox's Quest for the Rings game *is part board game, part video game, and part adventure game.*

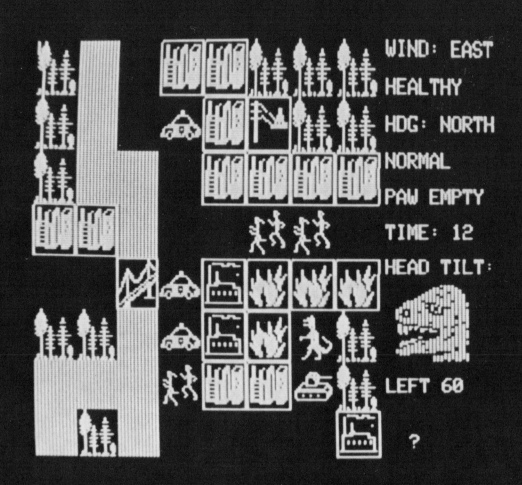

Crush, Crumble, and Chomp! *lets you*
play the part of a monster and
choose a major city to destroy.

a major city (such as San Francisco, New York, or Tokyo) that you'd like to eat for lunch. When the game begins, you can chase and trample the city's inhabitants or munch on the Golden Gate Bridge, the Pentagon, or the World Trade Center.

Automated Simulations' *Tuesday Morning Quarterback* is an unusual adventure. Instead of becoming a wizard or warrior you become the coach — and captain! — of a pro football team. In the huddle you call the team's plays. You get to choose from seven running plays, eight pass patterns, and an option play. On defense, you have six different formations and defensive plays. As in a real game, you have to think up a winning strategy, move fast, and watch out for pass interceptions, penalties, and costly fumbles.

In Synergistic Software's *Odyssey*, you are stuck on a tropical island, complete with steep mountains, a mysterious lake, exotic shops where you can barter for supplies, and villages full of unfriendly natives. When the game begins, you try to assemble an army, then you journey across the island looking for ancient treasures. Games of *Odyssey* can last for four hours and longer.

In On-Line Systems' *Cranston Manor*, you are whisked to the deserted town of Coarsegold. Coarsegold was destroyed by the cruel and greedy miser "Old Man Cranston," who finally died and left his treasure buried inside his mansion. Your mission is to find the treasure, carry it away, and use it to revive the little town.

Finally, in Krell Software's *Time Traveller* game, you take a time machine into the past looking for fourteen rings of magic. You search for the rings in Egypt at the time of the pharaohs, in Russia at the time of the Bolshevik Revolution, in Palestine during the Crusades, and in the United States during the Revolutionary War.

Each ring that you find gives you fantastic new powers that aid you in your search for additional rings. One ring turns you invisible, another makes you indestructible, a third lets you heal all the wounds you acquire on your journey. In each era of the past, you must fight off attackers, recruit allies and warriors, and buy or steal equipment and supplies.

CHAPTER 7

WHAT MAKES A GOOD GAME?

In the last four years, over 300 million copies of a thousand different electronic games have been sold. These include dozens of arcade video games; several video game machines and over 150 game cartridges; hundreds of hand-held games; and more than three dozen home computers, with hundreds of arcade games and adventure games you can run on them. What a rich variety to choose from!

But where do you start?

Among the thousand electronic games there are several superior ones — games with high quality pictures and sound effects and challenging, exciting action. But there are also dozens of bad games — literally, electronic junk. And the problem is, it's often hard in the store to tell the good games and bad games apart. Many bad games, like the good games, boast a dazzling show of sounds and lights. They beep and blink and look fantastic.

Then you take them home. In an hour or two, you're either bored silly or frustrated because your game is already broken. If you bought the game from a discount store, you may be stuck with it. The store may have a no-returns policy.

When shopping for video games, hand-held games, or tabletop games, the first rule of thumb is, don't pay any attention to the commercials you may see on TV. Advertising agencies go to a lot of trouble to jazz up the game action you see on TV, to the point where it is highly unrealistic.

So what do you do? When you get to the store, insist upon playing the game — several times. This is the quickest way to find out what a game is really like. The storekeeper should be agreeable to your doing this. If he or she isn't, find another store.

When you play the game at the store, what do you look for? First, note how the game is made. Is the plastic rugged-looking and durable? Are all the game labels in place? Is the paint job neat or sloppy? If the manufacturers didn't make the outside of the game look attractive, you can bet the inside — which you can't inspect — is no better.

Most important of all, look carefully at the game's display and test the game's sound effects. Is the display big and easy to read and follow? Are the figures in the display realistic? Is the display bright, or do you have to squint to make out the action?

How about the sound? Loud beeps and buzzes are startling and exciting at first. But could you — or your family — spend hour after hour listening to these noises?

Psychologists have shown that repetitive, loud noises cease to be interesting after a while. Our brains either tune them out or the noises make us irritated and angry.

Next, take a hard look at the game itself. The game is electronic and has a computer inside. But this alone doesn't make it worth the high price tag that most electronic games carry with them. Many electronic games are just fancy copies of non-electronic games that are often a good deal cheaper — certain strategy games and board games, for instance. Is it necessary for you to have a computer tell you a number, when you can just roll some dice? Or have a computer tell you your next move, when you could just as easily draw a card from a well-shuffled deck? Or play on a digital display, when an old-fashioned playing board is bigger, more colorful, and features real-looking game pieces made of inexpensive cardboard and plastic? Ask yourself whether you really need a computer to play a particular game, or whether a non-computer version might do just as well — or better.

Also, be sure to look through the game's instruction booklet while you're still at the store. Will you need any special attachments or game cartridges that don't come with the basic game? Is there anything to assemble? Are there any special requirements you should know about before you buy the game?

As to the directions themselves, is the booklet easy to understand? Is it complete, clear, and interesting looking? Again, a clue to whether the game is good or not is the quality of its instruction booklet. If the booklet is incomplete or hard to read, you should take an extra-long look at the game before you spend money on it.

Many electronic games run on batteries. These get used up and need to be replaced. Electronic games drink up battery "juice" like thirsty elephants at a watering hole. Also, it is very easy to leave a game and forget that the power is turned on. Then, hours later, when you come back to the game, you find a dead battery and a dead game. One way to avoid this is to get a game with an automatic power down. With this feature, an electronic game will automatically shut down a few minutes after you have stopped using it. Another thing to watch for is a game with a "reminder beeper." When you stop using a game with this feature, every thirty seconds it reminds you it is still turned on by beeping at you.

An AC adapter (known as an "adapter clip" for 9-volt transistor batteries) will let you plug your game into the wall and completely bypass batteries. Also, a battery recharger will let you recharge permanent batteries inside the game or regular batteries placed inside the recharge unit. If you decide to buy either of these pieces of equipment, pay careful attention to matching the game up with the proper adapter or recharge unit. There are dozens of units available, for batteries from 3 to 9 volts. The wrong unit will destroy your game and void your game's warranty — the guarantee from the manufacturer that they will repair a defective game during a certain limited period.

Finally, it's important to shop around for games. From one store to the next, prices on a single game can vary from $10 to $30 or more. Also, look for games made by reputable companies. The biggest names in electronic games are Atari, Magnavox, Mattel, Texas Instruments, Milton Bradley, Parker, Coleco, Ideal, and Selchow & Richter (the people who make *Scrabble*). These companies have been in the game business the longest time, and they distribute the largest number of games and game cartridges. In general, you can expect good games, lots of additional game cartridges, and good support from these manufacturers. And you'll need the support. If your game breaks, you will probably have to send it to the manufacturer to be repaired. Very few stores — especially department stores and discount stores — will repair electronic games.

CHAPTER

5

GAME STRATEGIES: HOW TO BE A WINNER

When you go to an electronic game arcade, you're sure to run into some hotshot who can play a single game for half an hour or longer and build up an incredible score of millions of points. Do you ever wonder how this player got so good? The answer is simple: *practice*.

But practice takes quarters. Lots of quarters. Does this mean that to become an expert you have to be rich?

Not at all. If you had a thousand quarters to get good at a particular game, there wouldn't be any pressure on you to improve in a hurry. You might keep playing and playing, but never get any better. Long before you spent your thousand quarters you'd be tired of playing the game.

People who have become experts aren't rich. But they do have a secret: they have a game allowance. They get the allowance for doing chores or part-time jobs. The allowance usually is anywhere from $2 to $5 a week. This gives enough quarters but not too many. The supply is limited. There is lots of pressure to learn the rules of a new game quickly and get good fast — before the quarters run out.

■ *Zapping Space Invaders*

It's high noon in Dodge City. Two gunfighters emerge from the shadows and stand facing each other, 50 feet (15 m) apart. For a moment, nothing happens. Each man is trying to size up his opponent. Then the silence is broken by gunfire. When the smoke clears, one man is lying crumpled up on the hard, sunbaked clay of the street. The other man places his gun in his holster and casually swings open the doors of the saloon.

This expert gunfighter learned long ago that when he faces a deadly opponent, he must immediately size him up. Estimating the opponent's major strengths and weaknesses requires the gunfighter to concentrate and be totally alert.

In a similar way, the expert game player learns quickly to size up a new game. When reading the game instructions for the first time, he or she is already looking for clues to the machine's strengths and weaknesses. Like a good gunfighter, electronic games can be fast as lightning. But both have a certain style — a regular way of acting — that can be used against them.

In electronic games, asteroids, aliens, spaceships, and attacking spiders all zip across the screen. But they usually zip along the same paths, at the same speed, in the same direction, or in the same pattern. They may be fast, but they are not smart. Their speed and numbers make them deadly, not their intelligence.

If you pay careful attention, you will see how they begin to repeat themselves, how certain portions of the game keep happening over and over. Learning these patterns makes the game predictable. This is the key, because once you can predict your enemy's next move, you can jump two steps ahead and outsmart him or her.

For example, if a purple dragon always enters the game after you've blasted the orange troll, then you can be ready either to flee or to blast the purple dragon. In every type of electronic game, when you know what happens next, you can get extra points and survive inside the game world a little longer.

Remember Bill Heineman, the teenager from the Los Angeles area who won the First National *Space Invaders* Competition in

1980? Bill didn't score 165,200 points because he had a superfast FIRE button finger, or because he is a genius. And he didn't win merely because he had spent hours playing *Space Invaders* at game arcades and on the Atari home video game. He won because he had noticed certain regular patterns in the *Space Invaders* game, and he had figured out a system to avoid destruction and shoot down more invaders at the same time.

The system wasn't even complicated. At each game reset, Bill moved his game figure along the bottom of the screen, from the extreme left to the extreme right. As he moved, he blasted the first line or two of oncoming invaders. When he reached the extreme right of the screen, he destroyed the invaders' rightmost column. He then flashed to the extreme left of the screen and began destroying invaders, column by column. Using this system, Bill could knock out an entire squadron of invaders plus a bonus ship in less than sixty seconds. Bill wiped out squadron after squadron, just following the same set of steps, over and over.

Bill and other expert players figure out foolproof systems that work so perfectly they can build up unbelievable scores. But not all systems have to be foolproof to let you get your money's worth from a game or score lots of points.

Also, each game is different. Bill, for example, tried to use parts of his *Space Invaders* system to beat the Atari *Asteroids* game. He flopped. When he blasted an alien invader, that particular invader was gone for good. But when he blew up an asteroid, its fragments became mini-asteroids. Each mini-asteroid was capable of destroying his spaceship. He had scored points, but he hadn't eliminated the danger.

■ *An Insider's View*
It's true that each electronic game is different and that different types of electronic games are different. You need practice, luck, skill, and a clever system to beat a good hand-held game, video game, or arcade game. And you can't excel at adventure games unless you think logically and are a master at solving puzzles and riddles.

Still, there are similarities among electronic games, the most important being that they are all the same on the inside. All the action, sound effects, and game characters are produced by a program running on a tiny computer inside the game. And what is a program? Just a sequence of steps the computer must follow, one after the other, over and over again.

The problem is that most game programs are long and complicated. And they were thought up by the most clever game designers in the world.

You can't drill a hole in a person's head to discover what he or she is thinking. And you can't pry open an electronic game and study its program. The program is not in English, but in a long, snakelike string of electrical pulses — blips of energy — coded in the computer's language telling the computer what to do.

However, there are ways to learn about the game program without tearing the machine part. Just as psychologists study people's behavior to learn more about their brains, good game players study the behavior of games to understand the game programs. Game programs aren't infinitely complex. They have to be small in order to fit inside a computer's memory circuits. Even the most ingenious, most complicated games begin to repeat themselves. Patterns and repetition — these form the basis for the game program and can serve as your keys to beating the game.

■ *Smarter Games*

Watching for patterns and repetition in a game, in order to figure out a system, can help you become expert at playing the game. But it is getting harder and harder to detect patterns and repetition in electronic games. As computer circuits continue to shrink, it becomes possible for game designers to squeeze bigger and craftier game programs into the tiny computer chips inside the game. As a result, electronic games are getting smarter and more difficult to beat.

For example, experts at Atari's *Asteroids* game learned that whenever enemy flying saucers appeared, they could hide their spaceship behind an asteroid. Then they would ambush the saucers. But no longer. Atari's *Asteroids Deluxe* game has "smart" flying saucers. Aware that your spaceship may be lurking behind an asteroid, these saucers first blow up each asteroid they encounter. If your ship is there, then they blow you up, too.

And in another game, Williams Electronics' *Star Castle*, there are "smart" space mines that seem to know where your spaceship is. If you aren't careful, within a few seconds of play the killer mines can track down your ship and destroy it.

How can you beat electronic opponents that always seem to know where you are? The key here is to try not to be fooled by the illusion of intelligence. For the next few years, even the smartest electronic games will still be dumb by human standards. Computers still aren't small enough or powerful enough for game designers to build electronic spaceships, dragons, or football players that are truly intelligent. Also, even with infinite computer power and infinite computer memory, we still don't understand human intelligence well enough to copy it in an electronic game. Besides, game designers are always forced to stay within a tight budget. Wherever possible, they have to make compromises and economize, or their games would be too expensive to produce. So, instead of real intelligence, they make games with the illusion of intelligence.

For example, the "smart" mines in *Star Castle* do not really know where you are. They only know what general direction your ship is in — north, south, east, or west. Then they head in that direction. The mines *seem* to know where your ship is because they move fast and because the computer re-aims each mine thirty-eight times a second.

The enemies and villains in good electronic games move so fast and act so smart, they can be frightening. This is exactly what the game designer intended. As soon as the game begins, you're running scared.

But if you realize that your electronic opponent's intelligence is faked — that it is just a clever illusion — you can stop being fooled by the designer's programming tricks and start looking for the patterns and repetitions in the designer's program.

CHAPTER 9

ELECTRONIC GAMES OF THE FUTURE

All the experts agree — we are in the middle of an electronic games revolution. No one knows for sure what kinds of games we'll see only five or ten years from now, but we can guess. Here are some of the key areas where electronic games are changing and improving. Be sure to watch these areas closely, and be ready for some amazing developments.

- *Pictures*
Computer scientists, artists, and filmmakers are getting computers to invent colorful, moving pictures out of such flimsy abstractions as light, shadow, texture, and contour. And the pictures look like the real thing — jagged mountains, murky green rivers, sleek fighter planes, and orbiting space stations. These highly realistic, highly detailed pictures will soon show up on electronic games, under the control of the computer and you.

In the meantime, there are lots of other developments to watch for, including games played on 7-foot (2.1-m) picture screens; games played on a flat TV screen on your wrist; and colorful, holographic pictures that are so realistic you can see over the wall of a game castle if you stand on your chair.

■ 55 ■

■ *Sound Effects*

Computers already produce artificial voices for electronic games. Although they can be very realistic, people seem to prefer machines that sound like machines — deep, mechanical voices like those of science-fiction robots.

In the future, you will be able to choose the voices used in the electronic game — anything from Darth Vader to Woody Woodpecker. And you'll be able to mix these voices with an electronic copy of your own voice.

Present-day games produce music, but only in the form of simple tones or ear-splitting sound effects. Future games will let you choose music that sounds like it came from your favorite musical instrument, whether it is a harmonica or a bass guitar. And you will be able to give orders to the game verbally — just like Captain Kirk shouting commands from the bridge of the *Enterprise* or a hockey coach barking orders to the team from the side of an ice rink.

■ *Game Worlds*

What else can you watch for? Look for games to come in new shapes and sizes — big, arcade game cockpits that you enter like the cockpit of the Space Shuttle, and portable games that you strap to your waist and that come complete with a miniature mike and earphones.

Look for multiplayer, multimachine games. Huge numbers of small computers may one day be linked into worldwide gaming "Olympics." You might even play in an international tournament

In the near future, you will enter a game "cockpit" or control room. Game controls, screens, and speakers will be everywhere.

while sitting on the floor of your living room. Your game will be linked with other games all over the planet by microwave transmissions bounced off satellites in earth orbit.

Today's electronic games are all isolated, one-shot machines. Watch in the future for huge, sprawling "game parks" — electronic Disneyworld-type places with nonstop, long-playing adventures for everyone. And watch for whole families of games that take you on lots of different exciting adventures inside the same game world.

The worlds inside today's adventure games are populated with what are known as NPCs — non-player characters. These are characters dreamed up by the Game Master to aid and challenge the real, human players and make the game world more interesting. Yet present-day computer-created NPCs are like puppets or shadow creatures. They are not lifelike enough to be truly frightening or become real allies or enemies.

But coming out of the laboratories are modern-day Frankenstein creatures known as *artificial intelligences*. These intelligences are not big hulking zombies, like the creatures of fiction, but computer programs that can think, reason, and solve problems. In the future, watch for electronic games populated with these artificial intelligences — creatures that are so unpredictable and clever that you'd swear they were real.

In fact, as farfetched as it may seem, these creatures may eventually become real. Some of today's most respected computer scientists have already speculated about "ultra-intelligent" computers that will become a new species of life on our planet. In this sense, the creatures we meet in today's electronic games are already real, but extremely primitive versions of the creatures we'll someday meet.

But this makes one wonder. If electronic games are just the beginning of live electronic creatures of the future, what happens when those creatures get tired of playing games? What if they decide to leave the game world and join us in the real world?

GAME MANUFACTURERS

This is only a partial listing of game manufacturers. It includes companies
that are well established and produce some of the best games.

■ *Hand-held, Tabletop, and Board Games*

Coleco Industries, 945 Asylum Avenue, Hartford, CT 06105. *Head-to-Head Baseball, Head-to-Head Football.*

Fidelity Electronics Ltd., 8800 N.W. 36th Street, Miami, FL 33178. *Sensory Voice Chess Challenger, Backgammon Challenger.*

Ideal Toys Corporation, 184-10 Jamaica Avenue, Hollis, NY 10010. *The Generals, Flash, Electronic Detective, Maniac.*

Kenner Products, 1014 Vine Street, Cincinnati, OH 45202. *Live Action Football, Redline.*

Mattel Electronics, 5150 Rosecrans Avenue, Hawthorne, CA 90250. *Football 2, Basketball 2, Brain Baffler, Soccer, Auto Race.*

Mego Corporation, 41 Madison Avenue, New York, NY 10010. *Fabulous Fred, Pocket-sized Time Out Games — Toss-Up; Fireman, Fireman; and the Exterminator. (Silly, fun games.)*

Milton Bradley Company, MB Communications, P.O. Box 2209, Springfield, MA 01101. *Pocket Simon, Microvision, Comp IV.*

Parker Brothers, 50 Dunham Road, Beverly, MA 01915. *Bank Shot Electronic Pool, Stop Thief!, Split Second, Merlin.*

Selchow & Richter Company, 2215 Union Boulevard, Bay Shore, NY 11706. *Scrabble Lexor Computer Word Game.*

Tryom, Inc., 23500 Mercantile Road, Beachwood, OH 44122. *Chess System III, Chess Traveler, Omar (backgammon).*

■ *Video Games*

Atari, Inc., 1265 Borregas Avenue, P.O. Box 427, Sunnyvale, CA 94086. Video computer system, game cartridges.

Magnavox (N.A.P. Consumer Electronics Corp.), P.O. Box 6950, Knoxville, TN 37914. Odyssey^2, game cartridges.

Mattel Electronics, 5150 Rosecrans Avenue, Hawthorne, CA 90250. Intellivision, game cartridges.

■ *Home Computers*
  Apple Computer Company, 10260 Bandley Drive, Cupertino, CA
    95014. Apple II Plus.
  Atari, Inc., 1265 Borregas Avenue, P.O. Box 427, Sunnyvale, CA
    94086. Atari 400, Atari 800.
  Commodore Business Machines, 681 Moore Road, King of Prussia,
    PA 19406. VIC-20, PET, CBM.
  IBM, Corporate Information, Armonk, NY 10504. IBM Personal
    Computer.
  NEC Consumer Products, 130 Martin Lane, Elk Grove Village, IL
    60007. NEC PC-8001A.
  Radio Shack, 1300 One Tandy Center, Fort Worth, TX 76102. TRS-
    80, Model III, TRS-80 Color Computer.
  Sinclair Research Ltd., 50 Stanford Street, Boston, MA 02114. ZX-
    80, ZX-81.
  Texas Instruments, Inc., Consumer Relations, P.O. Box 53, Lub-
    bock, TX 79408. TI 99/4A.

■ *Adventure Machines*
  Atari, Inc., 1265 Borregas Avenue, P.O. Box 427, Sunnyvale, CA
    94086. *Adventure, Warlords.* (Atari video computer system
    game cartridges.)
  Magnavox (N.A.P. Consumer Electronics Corp.), P.O. Box 6950,
    Knoxville, TN 37914. *Quest for the Rings.* (Odyssey² video
    game and board.)
  Mattel Electronics, 5150 Rosecrans Avenue, Hawthorne, CA 90250.
    Dungeons & Dragons. (Tabletop.)
  Milton Bradley Company, MB Communications, P.O. Box 2209,
    Springfield, MA 01101. *Dark Tower.* (Board, Tabletop.)

■ *Home Computer Game Programs*
  Adventure International, Box 3435, Longwood, FL 32750. *Pirate's
    Cove, The Count, Mystery Fun House, Ghost Town.*
  Adventure World, Box 914, North Chelmsford, MA 01863. *Jour-
    ney to the Center of the Earth, Enchanted Island Plus.*

Automated Simulations, Inc., Dept. TQ1, P.O. Box 4247, 1988 Leghorn Street, Mountain View, CA 94040. *Crush, Crumble, and Chomp!, Invasion Orion, Dragon's Eye.*

BudgeCo, 428 Pala Avenue, Piedmont, CA 94611. *Raster Blaster.* (Fabulous pinball game on the Apple computer.)

California Pacific Computer Company, 1623 Suite B, Davis, CA 95616. *Ultima, Apple-oids, Akalabeth...World of Doom.* (Many programs by Lord British, a foremost game designer.)

Creative Computing Software, P.O. Box 789-M, Morristown, NJ 07950. *Super Space Battle, Air Traffic Controller, Wumpus.*

Dakin5 Corporation, Level-10, P.O. Box 21187, Denver, CO 80221. *Dragon Fire.*

Hayden, 50 Essex Street, Rochelle Park, NJ 07662. *Backgammon, Mayday, Microsail, Sargon II (chess), Reversi (Othello).*

Krell Software, 21 Millbrook Drive, Stony Brook, NY 11790. *Sword of Zedek, Time Traveller.*

Med Systems Software, P.O. Box 2674-P, Chapel Hill, NC 27514. *Deathmaze 7000, Labyrinth, Asylum.*

Microsoft Consumer Products, 400 108th Avenue NE, Suite 200, Bellevue, WA 98004. *Microsoft Adventure.*

On-Line Systems, 36575 Mudge Ranch Road, Coarsegold, CA 93614. *Cranston Manor, Mission: Asteroid, Hi-Res Football.*

Personal Software Inc., 1330 Bordeaux Drive, Sunnyvale, CA 94086. *Zork: The Great Underground Empire.*

The Programmer's Guild, POB 66, Peterborough, NH 03458. *Lost Dutchman's Gold, Death Dreadnought.*

Quality Software, 666 Reseda Blvd., Suite 105, Reseda, CA 91335. *Fracas, Ali Baba and the 40 Thieves.*

Siro-Tech Software, 6 Main Street, Ogdensburg, NY 13669. *Wizardry.*

Sirius Software, Inc., 2011 Arden Way, #225A, Sacramento, CA 95825. *Gorgon, Pulsar II, Gamma Goblins, Autobahn.* (Many programs by Nasir, a foremost game designer.)

Synergistic Software, 5221 120th Avenue SE, Bellevue, WA 98006. *Odyssey, Doom Cavern, Wilderness Campaign.*

FOR FURTHER READING

■ *Books*

Ahl, David H., ed. *BASIC Computer Games (Microcomputer Edition)*. Morristown, NJ: Creative Computing Press, 1978.

——— *More BASIC Computer Games*. Morristown, NJ: Creative Computing Press, 1979.

Blumenthal, Howard J. *The Complete Guide to Electronic Games*. New York: New American Library, 1981.

Buchsbaum, Walter H. and Robert Mauro. *Electronic Games: Design, Programming, and Troubleshooting*. New York: McGraw-Hill, 1979.

D'Ignazio, Fred. *Computer Adventure Games: How to Create an Adventure of Your Own*. Rochelle Park, NJ: Hayden Book Company, 1982.

Heiserman, David L. *How to Design & Build Your Own Custom TV Games*. Blue Ridge Summit, PA: TAB Books, 1978.

Levy, David. *Chess and Computers*. Washington, D.C.: Computer Science Press, 1976.

Mateosian, Richard. *Inside BASIC Games*. Berkeley: Sybex, 1981.

Niven, Larry, and Steven Barnes. *Dream Park*. (SF novel about computer adventure-game park of the near future.) New York: Ace Books, 1981.

Saberhagen, Fred. *Octagon*. (SF novel about computer gaming and computer murder.) New York: Ace Books, 1981.

Spencer, Donald D. *Game Playing with BASIC*. Rochelle Park, NJ: Hayden Book Company, 1977.

Vinge, Vernor. "True Names." (SF novella about the future of computer adventure gaming.) Jim Frenkel, ed. *Binary Star #5*. New York: Dell Publishing Company, Inc., 1981.

■ *Magazines*

Ares. (Combined adventure game and magazine.) Simulations Publications Inc. (SPI), 257 Park Avenue South, New York, NY 10010. (bi-monthly; $16 per year.)

Compute! Small System Services, Inc., P.O. Box 5406, Greensboro, NC 27403. (monthly; $20 per year.) Games and game programming tips for the Apple, Atari, Radio Shack Color Computer, VIC-20, TI-99/4A, and ZX-81 computers.

Creative Computing. P.O. Box 789-M, Morristown, NJ 07960. (monthly; $20 per year.) Frequent reviews of all kinds of electronic games; complete listings of game programs for your home computer.

Different Worlds. (Non-computer fantasy & SF gaming magazine.) P.O. Box 6302, Albany, CA 94706. (monthly; $21 per year.)

Dragon. (Computer/non-computer fantasy & SF gaming magazine.) Dragon Publishing, TSR Hobbies (manufacturers of the original *Dungeons & Dragons* game), P.O. Box 110, Lake Geneva, WI 53147. (monthly; $21 per year.)

Moves. (A leading computer/non-computer war gaming magazine.) Simulations Publications, Inc. (SPI), 257 Park Avenue South, New York, NY 10010. (bi-monthly; $11 per year.)

Softside. Softside Publications, 6 South Street, Milford, NH 03055. (monthly; $30 per year.) Game reviews, game columns, and complete games for several brands of small computers.

The Space Gamer. (A leading magazine of computer/non-computer adventure gaming.) Box 18805-T, Austin, TX 78760. (monthly; $21 per year.)

INDEX